How the Morning and Evening Stars Came to Be

and Other Assiniboine
Indian Stories

How the Morning and Evening Stars Came to Be

and Other Assiniboine Indian Stories

Published by the
Montana Historical Society Press
in cooperation with the
Fort Peck Assiniboine and Sioux Tribes
and Fort Belknap Tribes

HELENA, MONTANA

Originally published as *How the Morning and Evening Stars Came to Be, The Crow,* and *Inkdomi and the Buffalo* in the Indian Reading Series by the Pacific Northwest Indian Program, Joseph Coburn, Director, Northwest Regional Educational Laboratory, Portland, Oregon

Cover drawing by Lisa Ventura
Design by DD Dowden

Revised edition copyright © 2003 by Fort Peck Tribal Library, Fort Peck Community College, P.O. Box 398, Poplar, Montana 59255

Distributed by the Globe Pequot Press, 246 Goose Lane, Guilford, Connecticut 06437, (800) 243-0495

Library of Congress Cataloging-in-Publication Data:
How the morning and evening stars came to be : and other Assiniboine Indian stories.
   p. cm.
Summary: A collection of three traditional tales collected at Fort Peck and Fort Belknap reservations in northern Montana, which were originally intended to teach young members of the tribe about their history and culture.
Contents: How the morning and evening stars came to be—The crow—Inkdomi and the buffalo.
ISBN 0-917298-96-9 (pbk. : alk. paper)
1. Assiniboine Indians—Folklore. 2. Legends—Montana—Fort Belknap Indian Reservation. 3. Legends—Montana,—Fort Peck Indian Reservation. [1. Assiniboine Indians—Folklore. 2. Indians of North America—Montana,—Folklore. 3. Folklore—Montana.]
E99.A84.H69 2003
398.2'089'9752—dc21

                    2003044596

This project was funded by an Enhancement Grant from the
Institute of Museum and Library Services awarded
to Fort Peck Tribal Library in 2001.
Additional funding was provided by
Assiniboine and Sioux Enterprise Community

* ★ *

CONTENTS

How the Morning and Evening Stars Came to Be

As told by Jerome Fourstar
Illustrated by Lisa Ventura

BEFORE THE WHITE MAN CAME, Indians followed Indian time. They had no clocks then. When they saw the morning star, they knew it was time to get up. The evening star meant it was time to go to bed.

This Assiniboine story tells how two brothers became the morning and evening stars in order to be useful to their people. It tells how they stopped an old lady witch, who could turn herself into a cow elk, from luring hunters into the woods and turning them into trees.

A long time ago, a man and his wife and their twin sons lived in a tepee in the woods. The man would go hunting and the woman tanned hides and made clothes.

One day when the boys were about 17 years old, their father told them they had to go on a long journey. Their mother prepared pemmican, dried meat, rosebuds and grease for their journey. Each boy also had a dog and a horse, which looked the same as his brother's.

The two boys left the next morning at daylight. They went southeast, traveling while the sun was high and straight over their heads. They came to a fork in the trail. One of the young men said to the other, "You take one of the trails, and I will take the other. Every so often we will look at our knives. If the blade of the knife is rusty, we will know that one of us is dead." So they both went off on different trails.

At sundown, the boy who took the left trail came to a tepee. The woman who lived there asked him where he was going. He told her he was going on a journey to explore the country.

The woman said he could stay and sleep there that night.
So the boy tied his horse to a tree, fed his dog and went to
bed. Early the next morning he had breakfast, packed his
buffalo robe on the horse and continued his journey.

That afternoon the boy saw a cow elk and chased it into the woods. When he entered the woods, it immediately became dark and he lost the cow elk.

The boy tied his horse to a tree and gathered some dry wood. He made a bonfire and started to eat his lunch. All of a sudden, he heard something coming through the brush. Out came an old lady! She said, "Grandson, I am cold. Can I sit by the fire and keep warm?"

The boy told her she could sit by the fire and keep warm. He offered her some of his food, but she said she wasn't hungry, just cold. She said, "Grandson, if you get sleepy, you can go to sleep. I will sit here and keep up the fire all night." So the boy covered himself with a buffalo robe and went to sleep.

After a long while, the old lady tried to find out if the young man was asleep. She said, "Look out, Grandson! The sparks are jumping toward you!" But he did not move. She took some of the fire and threw it toward him. Again she said, "Look out, Grandson! The sparks are jumping toward you!" But still he did not move, so she knew he was asleep.

The old lady
took a stick and
put one end of it
into her mouth
to wet it. Then
she took out her
medicine pouch
and stuck the
stick into it. She
touched the
young man with
the stick. He
turned into a
tree. Then she
went out and
touched the dog
and horse. They
also turned into
trees.

About this time the other twin looked at his knife and saw the rusty blade. He knew that his brother was dead. The boy turned his horse around and started back to the fork in the trail. When he got there, he started on the trail his brother had taken.

The young man went the very same way his brother had gone, with his dog leading the way. He stayed that night at the woman's camp and left early in the morning. He chased the cow elk into the woods and again it turned dark. He made camp at the very same place his brother had. Again, the old lady came, asking to warm herself. But he didn't trust her, and while pretending to sleep, he watched her through a hole in his buffalo robe. When she threw the sparks at him, he did not move.

He saw the old woman put a stick into her medicine pouch. She was about to touch him, when he jumped out of the way. He grabbed the stick and touched her with it. She turned into an old, crooked tree.

Then the boy told his dog to look for his brother. The dog went sniffing from tree to tree. Suddenly, the dog stopped and wagged its tail. The young man took the stick and touched the tree with it. It turned out to be his brother. The dog began sniffing again and stopped by another tree. This time it was the horse. The dog stopped by still another tree. So again the young man touched the tree with the stick. This time it was the dog.

After that, he took the stick and touched the other trees. They all turned out to be men and told the same story. They had all chased the cow elk into the woods and had met the old lady. The young twins told the other men what had happened and that the old lady was a witch. All the men went back to where they had come from.

On their way home, the two brothers stopped at the tepee where the first woman had told each of them to stay. When she saw them both together, she knew they were twins. They stayed there that night, and started home the next morning.

By sundown the twins were home. They told their parents what had happened. Their father told them, "From this day on, you two are going to be useful to the people." He said to one son, "You will go in the direction where the sun comes up. There you will stay. You will be the morning star. The people will know it is time to get up when they see you."

He told the other boy, "You will go toward the direction that the sun sets. And that is where you will stay. You will be the evening star. The people will watch you at dusk. When you disappear on the horizon, the people will know it is time to go to bed."

That is how the morning star and the evening star came to be in the sky. And from that day on, nobody turned people into trees.

The Crow

As told by Richard Blue Talk
Illustrated by Joseph D. Clancy, Sr.

INKDOMI IS A LEGENDARY FIGURE IN THE ASSINIBOINE CULTURE. He takes a role similar to the Blackfeet's Napi. Although Inkdomi claims to be the Creator of all things, he really is a trickster and a liar. Often, he takes the form of different animals and birds in order to play tricks on people. He does both good and bad things.

Stories about Inkdomi have been passed on from generation to generation, and many times one story will have several versions. Some of the stories are humorous and others are more serious. This story tells how Inkdomi, in the form of Eagle, turned Crow black.

A long time ago, Crow was a beautiful bird. He had a good singing voice.

Crow was very proud of himself. He would fly around and show off his beautiful feathers.

The other birds tried to talk to him, but he wouldn't pay any attention to them.

One day, Inkdomi, in the form of Eagle, wanted to say something to Crow. But Crow wouldn't have anything to do with him.

That made Eagle angry at Crow. Eagle said, "I will take away your beautiful voice and change the color of your feathers."

Eagle flew high into the air and then flew down towards Crow. As Eagle came close to Crow, Crow's feathers turned black and he lost his beautiful voice.

To this day, the crow is black and its voice sounds funny.

Inkdomi and the Buffalo

As told by Jerome Fourstar
Illustrated by Douglas Runs Through

IN THIS SECOND INKDOMI STORY, Inkdomi's greed proves
to be his undoing.

Once, long ago, while Inkdomi was on a journey, he saw
a herd of buffalo. He had been walking for two days
without anything to eat and was very hungry.

Inkdomi began to think how he could kill one of the
buffalo. Finally, he had an idea. As he walked toward the
buffalo, he started to cry. The leader asked Inkdomi why he
was crying. Inkdomi said, "The enemy killed my whole
tribe. I am the only one left. My brothers, if you would
help me, we could go and kill the enemy."

The leader asked Inkdomi how they could help him.
Inkdomi said, "You can run fast and are strong. You can
overtake the enemy and kill them." The buffalo agreed to
help. Inkdomi said, "First, you must close your eyes and
follow me as I sing with my gourd. When I say to charge,
all of you run as fast as you can. But your eyes must be
closed." Inkdomi led the buffalo toward a high cliff. As they
got close, he said, "All right, charge!" Inkdomi threw himself
over the edge of the cliff. All of the buffalo followed, killing
themselves when they hit the bottom.

Inkdomi had lots of meat then. As he skinned the buffalo, a lame fox came along and said, "Can I help you, my brother? I am so hungry. I would like to help you so we could eat some of the meat right away."

Inkdomi said, "No, first take some tripe to the creek and wash it. We will eat it later."

Inkdomi gave the fox some tripe. When the fox got to the creek, he quickly washed the tripe and ate it all up. He went back and told Inkdomi a big fish had taken the tripe away from him. Inkdomi gave him some more tripe to wash. Again the fox quickly washed the tripe, ate it up and came back with the same story.

He did this several times, and each time Inkdomi gave him more tripe. Finally, Inkdomi followed the fox to the creek. Again the fox quickly washed the tripe and ate it all up. About that time, Inkdomi went up to the fox and beat him up!

The fox left, crying as he walked along the creek. He met a wolf who asked him why he was crying. The fox told him what had happened.

The wolf said, "Don't worry, brother. We'll get even." The wolf called together all of the flesh-eating animals and told them what to do. So, the animals went to Inkdomi and told him some stories. Inkdomi fell asleep. While he was sleeping, they ate up all of his meat and left. When Inkdomi woke up, all of the meat was gone. Because of Inkdomi's trickery and greed, he wound up with nothing.

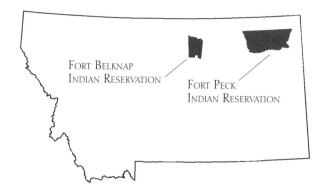

FORT BELKNAP
INDIAN RESERVATION

FORT PECK
INDIAN RESERVATION

About the Montana Assiniboine

"Known to our Canadian brethren as the Southern Assiniboine, we have lived in what is called Montana since the 1300s. Oral history tells us that we were the only Nation to use rocks to anchor or bank our lodges. The so-called teepee circles of rocks located throughout the Northern Plains are evidence of this. Archaeological evidence along the Canadian/American border in Montana is dated 1400 to 1600. Evidence exists of our ties to the Mound Builders of The Big River (Mississippi River). The evidence that the Assiniboine descended from the Yanktonai is from some Sioux in the 1600s. This Red Bottom Assiniboine Chief believes it is time to correct this wrong writing. I say we have been here since 1300s, this may be our second sojourn to this area, possibly third. Stories retained are proof of this. The Sioux story of the 1600s may have been true. Some of the Yanktonai may have joined the Assiniboines, but this story is not the beginning of the Assiniboine Nation."

Robert Four Star, Chief Buffalo Stops Four Times, RED BOTTOM ASSINIBOINE, APRIL 2003

Tribal members hunted buffalo and other game, fished the rivers and lakes, and gathered the many roots and fruit that the land provided. Active and sophisticated participants in the fur trade, they were known for pitting various fur companies against one another to further tribal interests. Small pox epidemics in the 1780s, 1800s, and 1830s ravaged the tribe, and death from disease reduced the tribe to four hundred families by 1838. Their small population led them to make alliances with other tribes, including the Cree and the Yanktonai Sioux. Today, members of the Assiniboine live on both the Fort Peck and Fort Belknap reservations in northern Montana and on several reserves in Saskatchewan and Alberta.

The stories published here have helped keep Assiniboine culture alive. Traditionally told around the fire on cold, winter evenings, stories like these were intended to help educate young tribal members about their history and culture. Children learned the stories from their elders, and, in their turn, passed them along to their children. Through this book these stories are now available to a new generation of Assiniboine children on the Fort Peck and Fort Belknap Indian Reservations and to children everywhere who are interested in learning about the traditional values and lifeways of the Assiniboine.